māori
art
for kids

For our mums:
Sandra (Morgan) Noanoa and
Sylvia (Alanson) Heke

māori art for kids

By Julie Noanoa with photography by Norm Heke

craig potton publishing

contents

tīmatanga kōrero
introduction

Māori art, the indigenous art of Aotearoa/New Zealand, is constantly evolving, embracing traditions of the past while drawing on contemporary culture and society. The information shared in this book is intended to enhance general knowledge of Māori culture through the artists' work and to encourage children to become actively involved.

This book is ideal for anyone interested in learning about Māori art and culture; educators working with children in schools or the community; and especially children engaging with aspects of Māori culture through practical activities.

The suggested art project supplies are readily available from art and craft supply shops, supermarkets and your own home recycling. It helps to organise all the materials and tools before you start your chosen project.

General Suggestions and Tips

‣ Be innovative by incorporating your own ideas, style, materials and colour choices when making your projects.

‣ Wear old clothes, especially when using paint and glue.

‣ Always use non-toxic paint and glue.

‣ Protect work surfaces with a waterproof cover.

‣ Be safe with scissors by cutting away from yourself.

‣ Adult assistance is advised when using tools and appliances, especially for younger children.

Notes

It is important to acknowledge that there are differences in cultural practices, beliefs and artistic design, as well as variances in language dialect between the many iwi (tribes) and hapū (sub-tribes) of Aotearoa/New Zealand.

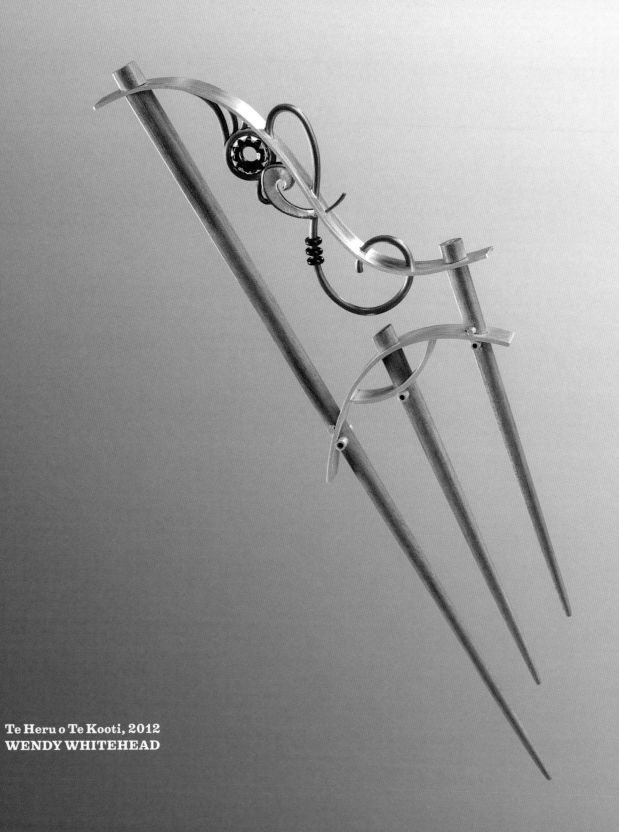

Te Heru o Te Kooti, 2012
WENDY WHITEHEAD

Wendy Whitehead, Fine Art Jeweller

The title of this work is *Te Heru o Te Kooti*. It was inspired by heru of old and the Judith Binney book *Redemption Songs: A Life of Te Kooti Arikirangi Te Turuki*. Traditional elements of shape (curve), decoration (manaia) and material (wood) sit together with the modern media of metal, glass and rubber. I was able to honour a traditional, beautiful, functional object with a contemporary look. I like the exaggerated size of the manaia (stylised figure), which makes a visual statement, giving the wearer a 'visual' voice that calls out to another world.

ARTIST'S ADVICE

'Feed and cultivate your mind – it is the garden of your creativity.'

heru decorative comb

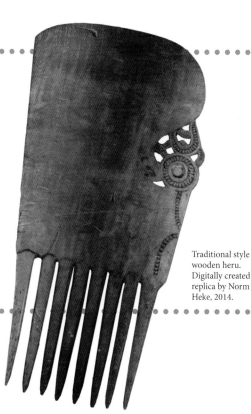

Traditional style wooden heru. Digitally created replica by Norm Heke, 2014.

About Heru

A person's head and hair are considered tapu (sacred) in Māori culture. Heru are a type of comb worn in the hair, and styles and the reasons for wearing them have changed over time. Like other valuable treasures, heru are handed down from generation to generation as family heirlooms. There are examples of heru made from solid pieces of wood and bone, while others are made of wooden pieces lashed together. Whalebone heru were the most highly valued.

In the past people could be recognised by the heru they were wearing because each one was unique. It was mostly men of chiefly status who wore heru, using them to secure their long hair that was twisted into a tight topknot on the head. Less commonly, women of chiefly status also wore heru. Today the trend has changed, and women and girls wear heru as a fashion accessory or on special occasions more often than men. Traditional heru or inherited heru still hold significant personal meaning to their owners.

Traditional Materials

Wood combs, bone.

Contemporary Materials

Metals, resin, plastics.

HOW TO MAKE A ...
heru decorative comb

1

Select a combination of diamantés, carefully arrange the selected pieces onto your comb the way you would like, then glue them on.

2

To create the long feathery tufts, strip strands from the feather's quill (mid section), leaving a small portion at the top, and repeat on the other side of the quill.

3

Ask an adult to help you carefully glue the pieces in place, using tweezers for small objects. Glue feathers to the back of your heru.

These heavenly heru have a matching slide comb each. The heru is useful for combing your hair and the slide comb can be worn as a fun hair accessory.

Materials & Tools

- plastic afro comb
- craft feathers
- diamantés
- scissors
- tweezers
- hot glue gun (ask an adult to help)
- slide comb (optional)

Alternative Materials

- Use fabric flowers.

Suggestion

- Bind the feathers to the comb with string instead of using hot glue.

Waka Maumahara, 2014
TODD COUPER

Todd Couper, Artist/Sculptor

This particular piece was carved as a memorial for my cousin Jeff who passed away some years ago. He was himself a skilled wood craftsman who strived for perfection in his own work and had a great appreciation for art. A long time ago he gave me some beautifully seasoned kauri to carve, so I made sure to do the wood justice and have used it for numerous artworks. My brother and I thought it would be a fitting gesture to use some of that wood to create a memorial piece to give back to the family.

A waka huia concept seemed appropriate for such an artwork because it not only served as a taonga (treasure) in itself, but its practical function as a vessel symbolised Jeff's legacy and encapsulated those memories within. His gift to me I can now pass back to his loved ones for them to always treasure. Much aroha to my uncle Futch and aunty Andrea, and to my cousins Tania and Paula and their families.

waka huia feather box

Traditional style waka huia.

About Waka Huia

Traditionally, waka huia were carved to house the personal possessions and adornments of rangatira (chiefs) and their families. Precious items such as feathers, combs, ear pendants and hei tiki were placed in a waka huia that was suspended from the rafters of the chief's whare (house). The underside was therefore visible and often carved with intricate detail.

The vessels are called waka huia because they were used to hold the feathers of the huia bird. Huia feathers were a particularly prestigious head adornment. A chief's head was very tapu (sacred), and this tapu extended to the taonga (treasures) that came into contact with the head. It was important to keep these special treasures safe and out of reach of others to ensure they were not mistreated or touched by anyone other than the chief.

Waka huia are still carved today by carvers and artists. Although styles and traditional tapu restrictions have changed over time, essentially waka huia are still used in a similar manner. Waka huia are prized artworks in their own right and the ideal place for anyone to keep their own personal treasures.

Traditional Materials

Wood, pāua shell.

Contemporary Materials

Resin, glass, stone.

waka huia feather box

1

To make the stamps, use a pen to trace around a bottle top onto craft foam. Cut out the circle and draw a design on top (see template on page 74 for examples).

2

Cut out your design. Cover the bottle top surface with strips of double-sided tape, remove the top of the tape and attach your design.

3

Draw the template for the waka huia (see page 74) onto a piece of craft card, making sure to mark out the dashed fold lines.

4

Cut out the template.

Crease along all the fold lines – this will help you construct the waka huia.

5

Make your own stamp pad with paint applied to a sponge, or paint directly onto the stamp with a brush. Stamp patterns over the flat waka huia base and leave to dry.

Apply glue to the tabs and join them to the base, with the exception of the lid tab which helps to keep the lid on.

This is possibly the most challenging project, as you have to get the dimensions of the template right. Make it easy by photocopying the template on page 74, scaled to the size you prefer.

Materials & Tools

▸ craft card
▸ colour or glitter
▸ glue stick
▸ double-sided tape
▸ stamp, craft foam
▸ recycled plastic bottle tops
▸ paint
▸ sponge or paint brush

Alternative Materials

▸ Recycle a small cardboard shoe box, painted and decorated with your handmade stamps.

Suggestion

▸ To add colour to your waka huia, brush a dye wash over the craft card and allow to dry before decorating.

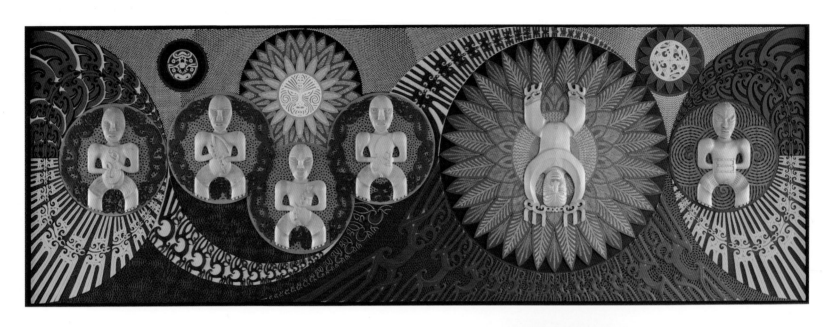

Te Wehenga o Rangi rāua ko Papa, 1975
DR CLIFF WHITING

Dr Cliff Whiting
Master Carver/Educator/Painter/Print Maker

Te Wehenga o Rangi rāua ko Papa tells the story of how the sky and earth became separated. Depicted in the wall panel from left to right are Tangaroa, god of the sea; Haumia, god of uncultivated foods; Rongo, god of cultivated foods; Tūmatauenga, god of war and people; Tāne, god of the forest; and Tāwhirimātea, god of the wind (shown in the enlarged detail). Tāne is represented upside down in the process of separating Ranginui (sky father) from Papatūānuku (earth mother).

In the story, the children of Rangi and Papa lived in the perpetual darkness created by their parents' locked embrace. The children desired to bring light into their world, prompted by a chance discovery that set in motion a plan to separate the parents, a plan opposed by Tāwhirimātea. After unsuccessful attempts by some of the brothers, the parents were eventually forced apart by Tāne.

Traditional style poupou.

poupou
carved wall panel

About Poupou

Poupou are the wall-mounted figurative carvings found inside a whare tīpuna (ancestral Māori meeting house). Each poupou is unique, representing an important ancestor and/or historic event of the iwi (tribe) it belongs to. Whare tīpuna, also known as wharenui, are located throughout Aotearoa/New Zealand. Different carving styles are evident in poupou from region to region.

A legend from the Ngāti Porou iwi explains the origin of carving through the adventures of Ruatepupuke, who discovered the house of Tangaroa deep below the sea while searching for his lost son. When Ruatepupuke left the house of Tangaroa he took with him examples of poupou and tekoteko (carved gable figures), bringing the art of carving to the world.

Traditional Materials

Native timber, including tōtara, rimu, pūriri, kauri and maire.

Contemporary Materials

Introduced wood suitable for carving, MDF board, metals.

HOW TO MAKE A...
poupou print

1

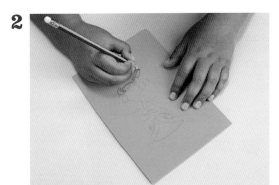

Fold the craft foam in the middle and cut it in half. Fold the white paper down the middle and cut to the same size as the craft foam.

2

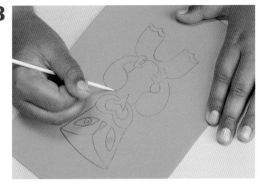

Choose a poupou example from page 71 to copy, or come up with your own style. Use a pencil to lightly draw your poupou onto the craft foam.

3

When you're happy with your drawing, press over all the pencil lines gently but firmly with a bamboo skewer to create an indented line.

4

Squeeze out a blob of ink onto a piece of scrap cardboard, and spread it to evenly cover the roller.

5

Spread a thin layer of ink over the craft foam base, reapplying ink to the roller as needed.

6

Centre the white paper over the foam base, lightly press it down and smooth with your hand for even coverage. Lift paper at one corner to reveal the finished print.

These poupou prints make great greeting cards for family or friends. To make the cards, trim around the entire edge of the dry poupou print, leaving a 10 mm margin. Glue the print to an A5 piece of paper and mount on one side of a piece of folded A4 black card.

Materials & Tools

- A4 craft foam sheet
- A4 white paper
- A4 black card
- sharpened pencil
- bamboo skewer or pointed stick
- water based ink and roller
- scrap cardboard
- scissors
- glue stick

Alternative Materials

- Use water based acrylic paint and a paint brush instead of ink and roller.

Suggestion

- Try a kōwhaiwhai design (see page 72 for examples) instead of poupou.

Kete Whakairo, 2003
SONIA SNOWDEN

18

Sonia Snowden, Master Weaver

The kete shown here is a lovely example of kete whakairo, one of many beautifully constructed creations by Sonia Snowden. Her woven works include tukutuku panels and kakahū (cloaks). Each strand of harakeke (flax) used to make this kete was carefully collected, prepared, softened and stripped by hand. The dark parts were dyed, while the lighter areas were left natural. Incorporated in the designs are Te Rā o Tainui (the sail of Tainui), Pāpaka (crab) and Kōwhitiwhiti (the dancing waters of Moananui-a-Kiwa). These woven patterns recall the journey of our tūpuna from Hawaiki nui, Hawaiki roa and Hawaiki pamamao, the ancient spiritual homelands from where Māori people migrated to Aotearoa/New Zealand.

ARTIST'S ADVICE

'The conservation and preparation of fibres is the most important part of weaving. Learn about your weaving fibres, patterns and techniques. Rāranga (weaving) proficiency means … practise, practise, practise.'

kete bag

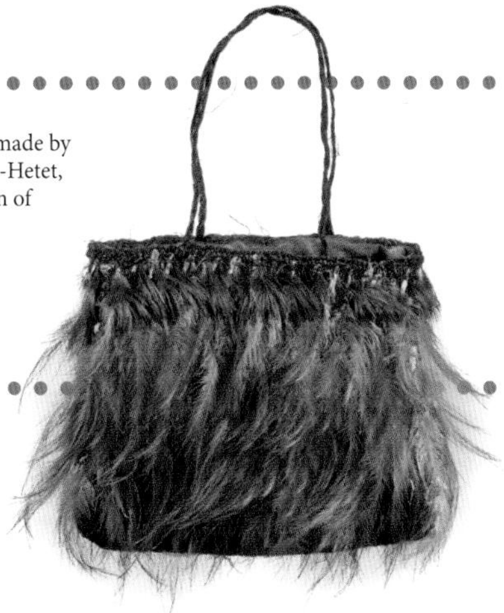

Kiwi feather kete made by Eranora Puketapu-Hetet, from the collection of Norm Heke.

About Kete

Kete are a type of bag or basket. In earlier times kete were important in everyday life for carrying and storing food. Plain open-weave baskets could be made quickly from strips of harakeke (flax). Kete were made and designed for specific purposes; for example a kete used for carrying kūmara would not be used to carry shellfish. A greater level of skill goes into preparing the various types of materials required to make traditional intricately crafted kete such as kete whakairo.

General patterns seen in kete include pātiki (flounder fish), poutama (stairway) and ruarua whetū (double star). Some kete are dyed with natural dyes, and to get a black dye a special type of mud called paru was used. Two examples of finely crafted kete are kete tāniko, which displays strong geometric patterns, and kete whakairo, made from finely woven strands of fibre.

Traditional Materials

Harakeke (flax), muka harakeke (prepared flax), kiekie, tī kōuka, kuta (reed), pīngao (sand dune grasses), toetoe, houhere (lacebark), native bird feathers, dyes – derived from natural plants, bark and special types of mud.

Contemporary Materials

Plastics, cotton, wire, copper wire, commercial synthetic dyes.

HOW TO MAKE A ...
kete bag

1

Lay out the coffee sack, and use a ruler and marker pen to draw a rectangle. Cut out two rectangles of the same size and shape.

2

Fold masking tape over the edges of both rectangles to stop the edges fraying, then turn any graphic or text you have chosen to face the inside.

3

Thread the embroidery needle. Pull an arm's length of wool through the needle and cut it, joining up the two ends by making a knot.

4

Sew down three sides leaving one side open. If the wool runs out, tie off the end, rethread the needle and continue from where you left off. Continue sewing down all three sides, filling in the gaps.

5

Once all three sides are sewn, turn the kete inside out to conceal the stitching.

6

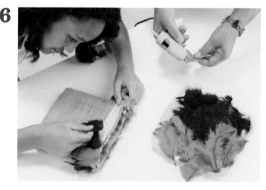

Attach feathers to the top edge with hot glue, but ask an adult to help. Make a plaited handle from recycled T-shirt material (see page 60) and sew it into the top inside corners of the kete.

Make your very own funky feathery designer kete,
to carry your trinkets or treasures.

. . . .

Materials & Tools

▸ feathers
▸ recycled coffee sack
▸ ball of wool
▸ plastic embroidery needle
▸ masking tape
▸ scissors
▸ marker pen
▸ hot glue gun (ask an adult to help)

Alternative Materials

▸ Substitute strong craft glue
  for hot glue.

Suggestion

▸ Stitch your name or Māori
  designs on your kete.

. . . .

Tinakori, 2006
NGĀTAI TAEPA

Ngātai Taepa, Artist/Tutor

He tirohanga tēnei ki ngā āhua matatini o Te Pitau a Manaia. Ki tēnei poupou, e rua ngā manaia e whakaatu nei i ngā kōrero e pā ana ki te hononga o te tuakana me te teina. Ko te ingoa o tēnei mahi ko *Tinakori* e maumahara ana ki te wā i hunuku te whakaaturanga toi o Tinakori, ki te wā hoki i tini te ingoa i a Tinakori ki a Page Blackie Gallery.

This 3D artwork features a kōwhaiwhai pattern called Te Pitau a Manaia. On the pou we have two manaia that show the relationship between an older and a younger sibling. This artwork is named *Tinakori*, and recalls the time when the Tinakori art gallery moved and changed its name from Tinakori to the Page Blackie Gallery.

ARTIST'S ADVICE

'Rapua te mea ngaro.'
(Seek that which is lost, not obvious.)
Nā Tāwhiao

kōwhaiwhai
scroll pattern

Traditional style kōwhaiwhai.

About Kōwhaiwhai

Kōwhaiwhai are well-recognised Māori motifs, often used in art, advertising media and design representing Aotearoa/New Zealand, and applied to everyday objects. Koru/pītau (see page 31) and kape form the basis of the geometrical kōwhaiwhai patterns. The kape is shaped like a crescent moon with the addition of regularly spaced circles. Kōwhaiwhai patterns are traditionally painted in whare tīpuna (ancestral meeting houses), pātaka (storehouses), on the prow of a waka (canoe) or the many forms of carving such as boat paddles or water containers.

Kōwhaiwhai in whare tīpuna are specifically designed for the iwi (tribe) the house belongs to, incorporating stories relevant to their history. Kōwhaiwhai are painted on the tāhuhu (ridgepole) of the house, stretching the length of the building. The kōwhaiwhai painted ridgepole represents the whakapapa (genealogy) of the iwi, from the main ancestor at the front of the house, going all the way to the back. Kōwhaiwhai patterns descend periodically on heke (rafters) from the ridgepole, and each heke connects with a poupou (ancestral figure).

Traditional Materials

Natural pigments, e.g. iron-rich powdered stone for red, charcoal for black or taioma (white clay) for white, mixed with shark oil as a fixative.

Contemporary Materials

Synthetic paints (e.g. acrylic, oil or water paints), inks, pencils, crayon, sculpture, stone, glass, plastic, carving, photography, design, clothing, ceramic.

HOW TO MAKE A ...
kōwhaiwhai container

1

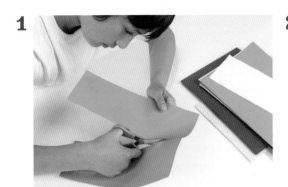

Fold a coloured A4 sheet in half lengthways and cut along the fold to make the base sheet. Repeat with a different coloured piece of paper to make the top sheet.

2

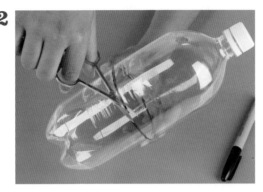

Measure the base sheet up against the bottle and draw a line with a marker pen right around it. Pierce and cut through the bottle with scissors following the marked line (ask for adult help if you need it).

3

Take the top sheet, fold it in half, then fold it in half again. On one side draw koru shapes in pencil, starting from the edges inward. Use an eraser if you make a mistake. See template on page 72 for ideas.

4

Carefully cut out the kōwhaiwhai shapes. When you've finished gently unfold the paper to reveal the geometric repeating and reflecting patterns you have created.

5

Paste the kōwhaiwhai sheet to the base with PVA glue, and leave to dry. Seal the paper by applying two coats of watered down PVA (2 parts glue to 1 part water) – allow to dry between coats.

6

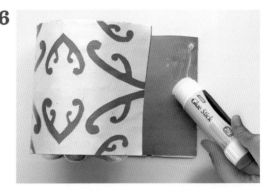

Tape the top cut edge of the bottle with masking tape to make a smooth edge. Glue the finished kōwhaiwhai pattern to the outside of the bottle with a glue stick. Fill your container with pens or pencils.

The patterns you use to make this kōwhaiwhai container will include elements of geometry such as reflection, rotation and symmetry. Most kōwhaiwhai have a manawa (heart) line that flows through the length of your pattern. See if you can find a manawa line in the pattern you make.

Materials & Tools

‣ recycled plastic drink bottle
‣ A4 coloured paper
‣ pointed scissors
‣ pencil
‣ eraser
‣ PVA glue
‣ glue brush
‣ masking tape
‣ glue stick

Alternative Materials

‣ Substitute a recycled plastic jar for the plastic drink bottle.

Suggestion

‣ Use the leftover pieces of koru shapes to decorate a greeting card.

Ipu Kākano (seed vessel), 2014
AMORANGI HIKUROA

Amorangi Hikuroa, Clay Sculptor

This artwork is called *Ipu Kākano*. I believe the role of an artist is to be the voice of their society, observing and harmonising with their surroundings. I make objects of beauty influenced by good form and line, stories old and new and everyday happenings. I look to the natural world for direction, to the simplicity and complexity of our environment, to fire, water, weather, the great oceans that link all lands, and the vast unknown universe.

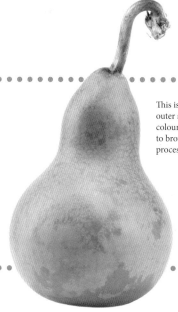

This is a dried hue (gourd), the outer shell hardened and the colour changed from green to brown during the drying process.

ipu container

About Ipu

Ipu is the general term to describe a container or vessel. Traditional containers were used for holding water, preserved food, serving dishes, pigments and dyes. The feathers of a bird preserved inside the container were attached as a label marker. The outer surface was sometimes decorated with etched kōwhaiwhai patterns. Other types of ipu are kumete (carved wooden bowls) and pātua, made from the inner bark of the tōtara or mānuka tree.

Hinepūtēhue is the female deity of hue, and the most common types of container used in the past were the hue/tahā or gourd, grown from seed. They were also used as a buoyancy device and as musical instruments. Gourds can be cultivated by skilled gardeners to create long, thin or widened forms. A gourd's outer surface when dried is hard and durable, so once the inside seeds are removed and the top cut off they make excellent storage containers. Today hue are mostly kept as ornamental objects.

Traditional Materials

Hue/tahā (gourd), tōtara bark, mānuka bark, seaweed, wood.

Contemporary Materials

Clay (uku), glass.

HOW TO MAKE AN ...
ipu container

1

Blow up the balloon and tie a knot at the end. Rest the balloon on top of a jar as a working surface. Spread a plastic table cover underneath your workspace to protect the surface.

2

Prepare a bowl full of the tissue paper torn into thin, even strips. Dilute PVA glue in a jar by mixing 2 parts glue to 1 part water.

3

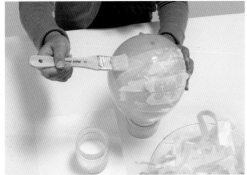

Paste strips evenly around the balloon, one strip at a time. Build up to at least seven layers – you don't need to wait for the glue to dry between layers. Flip the balloon regularly to apply layers at opposite ends.

4

To decorate, make koru or kōwhaiwhai patterns with string, and paste on with glue. Leave to dry completely. Once dry, cut the balloon's knot with scissors to deflate it.

Materials & Tools

▶ medium size balloon
▶ tissue paper
▶ string
▶ PVA glue
▶ water
▶ jar
▶ paste brush
▶ scissors
▶ plastic table cover

Alternative Materials

▶ Use recycled newspaper, or recycle the tissue paper from clothing patterns.

Suggestion

▶ Decorate with painted kōwhaiwhai patterns.

These make great decorative pieces to display on a shelf
or as a hanging ornament.

Hinetītama, 2011
NORM HEKE

Norm Heke, Photographer/Digital Artist

The central figure in this artwork is Hinetītama, the Dawn Maiden. In Māori whakapapa (genealogy) she was the first child to be born into the world. She is depicted here with her children in the golden glow of morning light, their garments provided by Tāne Mahuta (guardian of the forest). This portrait conveys the idea of growth and new life, similar to the meaning behind the koru form.

Two types of mature, unwound fern fronds make up the skirt worn by Hinetītama. One is a mamaku (black tree fern) and the other is a ponga (silver fern), a national symbol often used to represent New Zealand. The only garment that is real in this image is the bodice that the girl is wearing, made from muka (processed flax fibre) by weaver Kohai Grace. Everything else was digitally created by piecing together multiple photographs taken at different times and places, like a jigsaw puzzle.

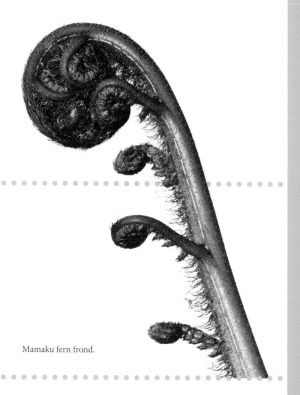

Mamaku fern frond.

koru
spiral form

About Koru

The coiled motif of the koru is a frequently used design in many Māori art forms. Another term for koru is pītau, which is also the name of the fern frond. As the fern grows, the tightly wound spiral unravels into a fully formed leaf, symbolising growth and renewal. The spiral shape occurs elsewhere in nature too, for example on shells.

The koru is the main element of kōwhaiwhai design, and today koru are a regular feature in advertising to represent Aotearoa/New Zealand. Māori and non-Māori artists have explored the koru extensively, experimenting with colour and shape, and adding design elements. The koru is applied on all types of surfaces in this country, including cups, clothing, shoes, paper and materials.

Traditional Materials

Carved into wood, bone, stone; painted with natural pigments.

Contemporary Materials

Metal, plastic, ceramics, clay, cardboard, cloth and vinyl.

31

HOW TO MAKE A ...
koru spiral

1

These pāua shells were collected from different beaches over a long period of time and taken to the beach to be photographed. Pre-rinsing the shells in the water helps to intensify their colour.

2

Draw out a koru shape in the sand with your hand or a stick as a guide to line up the shells. When complete, carefully smooth out the area around the shells with your hands.

3

When ready to take photos, zoom in to fill the camera frame with the subject. Try photographing from a variety of different angles. Early morning or late afternoon are good times of the day for photography, as the light falls across shapes creating shadows, adding form and richness to your image.

You could apply the idea of this koru shell photographic series to a whānau (family) walk in the bush, photographing interesting objects like fallen leaves.

Materials & Tools

▸ camera
▸ collected shells
▸ bucket

Alternative Materials

▸ Find and use stones, seaweed or driftwood at the beach.

Suggestion

▸ Print and frame your best photographs for display.

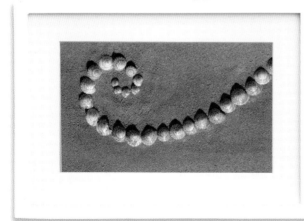
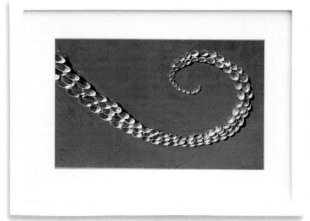

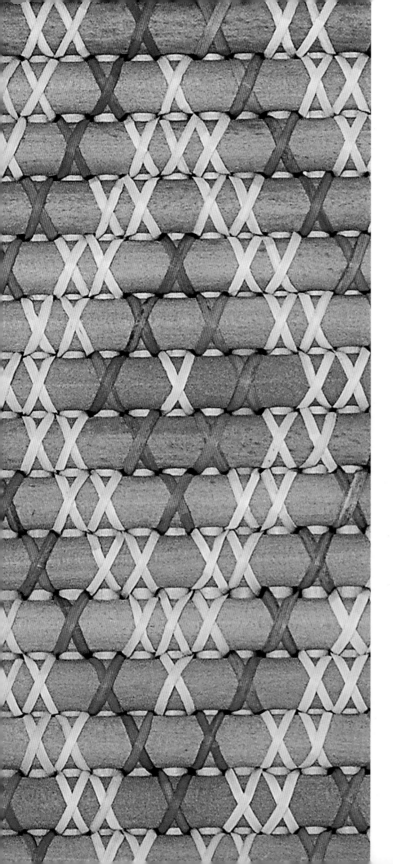

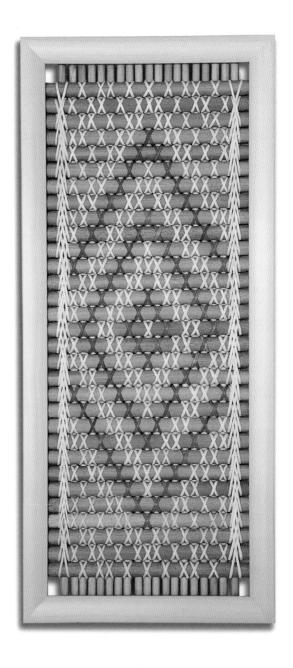

Pātikitiki, 2013
KOHAI GRACE

Kohai Grace, Weaver/Tutor

This tukutuku panel uses an old pattern called Pātikitiki. Pātikitiki is a group of stars near the Milky Way that were observed in traditional times for weather forecasting and determining favourable days for planting and fishing. 'Pātiki' is also the flounder fish. Perhaps the diamond motifs of the Pātikitiki pattern represent the shape or formation that is shared by both the stars (pātikitiki) and the fish (pātiki). Pātikitiki talks about success and prosperity that comes with good planning, resourcefulness and working cooperatively. I like the look of this pattern and how an old theme can continue to portray a relevant message or story for today.

tukutuku wall panel

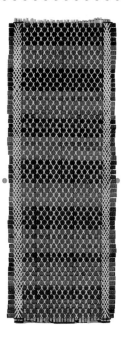

Traditional style tukutuku panel.

About Tukutuku

Traditional tukutuku are the lattice display panels inside whare tīpuna (ancestral meeting houses), usually located along the walls between the poupou and epa carving. They are an important part of the stories held inside the whare tīpuna. Tukutuku are identifiable by the geometric straight lines that dominate the design.

> The narrow, horizontal rods forming the front are called kaho tarai (Ngāti Porou) or kaho tara (Te Arawa). These were sometimes made from dry bracken fern stalks, or adzed laths of totara or rimu, and were lashed to vertical stakes of kakaho (flower stalks of toetoe) placed close together with the butt ends alternating with the flower ends to maintain a uniform width. Sometimes a round rod, tumatakāhuki, is laced up the middle on the front face of each panel. (Dougal Austin, 2014)

Decorative patterns were developed by intertwining dyed and undyed strips of soft leaves, which could be harakeke (flax), kiekie (ariel plant) or pīngao (sand dune grass). Today both contemporary and traditional tukutuku panels are used for individual decorative wall displays in homes or public buildings.

Traditional Materials

Toetoe stalks, pīngao, kiekie leaves – dyed with natural dyes or sun bleached.

Contemporary Materials

Bamboo, pampas grass, plastic, particle board, metal wire, wool, raffia, string, cardboard.

tukutuku wall panel

1

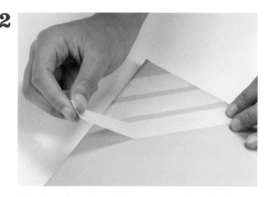

First plan your pattern by sketching ideas on paper (see designs opposite). Paint the entire surface of the canvas with your chosen base coat and leave to dry.

2

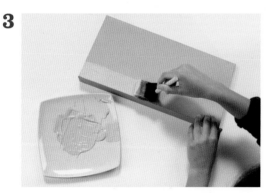

Cut lengths of masking tape and apply them to the canvas to cover the areas of your plan that won't be painted. Use a ruler if required. Continue taping until you have completed your pattern. This painting technique is called 'paint resist'.

3

Apply an even top coat of paint to the entire canvas. Allow it to dry before applying a second coat.

4

When the paint is thoroughly dry, carefully peel back the tape to reveal the pattern.

Materials & Tools

▶ canvas
▶ two colours of acrylic paint
▶ masking tape
▶ sponge brush or paint brush
▶ paper
▶ pencil
▶ ruler (optional)

Alternative Materials

▶ Recycle a shoe box lid instead of using canvas for the base.

Suggestion

▶ Using a hair dryer between coats speeds up the drying process.

These three linear tukutuku designs are called (from left to right): Kaokao (ready for challenges); Pātikitiki (a diamond shape reminiscent of a flounder); Poutama (ascending steps).

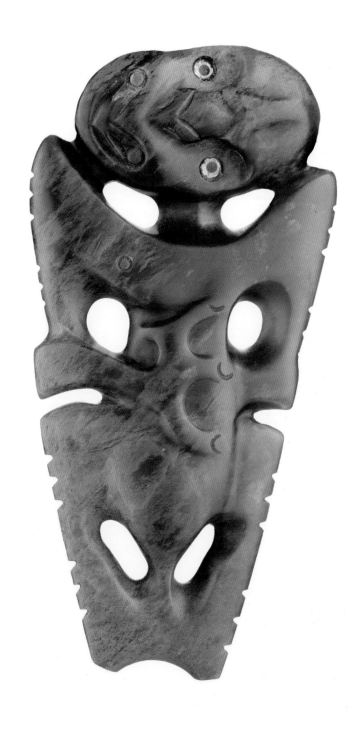

Hei Tiki I, 2013
LEWIS GARDINER

Lewis Tamihana Gardiner, Carver

Hei tiki are very individual – they have their own human characteristics so no two should be the same. When I design and develop hei tiki, the fundamental concepts for me are that it needs a head, a body and an interpretation of arms and legs. With this in mind there are no limits to how far you can push the hei tiki form. This allows me to move from traditional forms to a very contemporary design without losing the identity of the hei tiki. I tend to use mainly New Zealand pounamu as material for hei tiki, but once in a while I will use jade from overseas. It depends whether the character of the jade has something that makes it special; bright colours or a quality that justifies its use for hei tiki.

The process of carving a hei tiki has sped up dramatically through the introduction of diamond tools, grinders and burrs, reducing the making time to days rather than months. The new process gives it a machine look, with harder edges and sharper angles, with the final hand rubbing and finishing giving it a softer feel. The old process of working pounamu gave it a soft, smooth finish that is hard to replicate with modern techniques. The hei tiki is the most time-consuming pendant carvers can make. I name any hei tiki that is personal to the wearer, though some commisioned hei tiki are named by the client before I start, which is their way of making a connection to the piece.

Hei Tiki II, 2013
Lewis Gardiner

hei tiki
neck pendant

About Hei Tiki

The word 'tiki' is used widely throughout Polynesia for the human form. The word 'hei' in this context means something worn around the neck, therefore a hei tiki is a neck pendant in human form. People of all ages and cultures can be seen wearing hei tiki in Aotearoa/New Zealand, made from contemporary or traditional materials, and worn as everyday accessories or for a special occasion. The most highly prized hei tiki are made from pounamu or whalebone. Like many other important family taonga (treasures), hei tiki are often handed down from generation to generation, along with their own personalised name. Contemporary Māori artists create traditional and modern hei tiki, which are given names either by their maker or owner if they choose.

Traditional Materials

Whale tooth, whalebone, pounamu, muka (flax fibre), pāua shell.

Contemporary Materials

Metal, glass, plastic resin, found materials, pāua shell, polymer clay.

hei tiki neck pendant

1

Soften the clay to make it pliable by squeezing and rolling it with your hands on a flat surface.

2

Roll out a flattened oval piece about 5 mm thick. Press in the sides at the top third to create the neck shape.

3

Roll small pieces to make rounded strips that will form the eyes, arms, fingers, legs and mouth. Use the same colour if you prefer.

4

Gently press each shape onto the base (see the template on page 70).

5

Use the sharp end of a skewer to make decorative marks and lines. Make a hole in the top or side for threading string after baking.

6

Place the finished work on a foil-covered baking tray. Follow the baking instructions specific to your modelling clay – this hei tiki was baked at 130˚C for 15 minutes. When it's completely cool, thread the prepared hole with string.

These hei tiki examples show different styles
and colour combinations for you to try, or come up with your own design.

Materials & Tools

▸ oven-bake modelling clay
▸ bamboo stick
▸ oven

Alternative Materials

▸ Use cardboard instead of clay, layering a base with shapes to make features, arms and legs.

Suggestion

▸ Experiment by blending different colours of modelling clay, for example, combining blue and red makes purple, red and yellow makes orange, yellow and blue makes green.

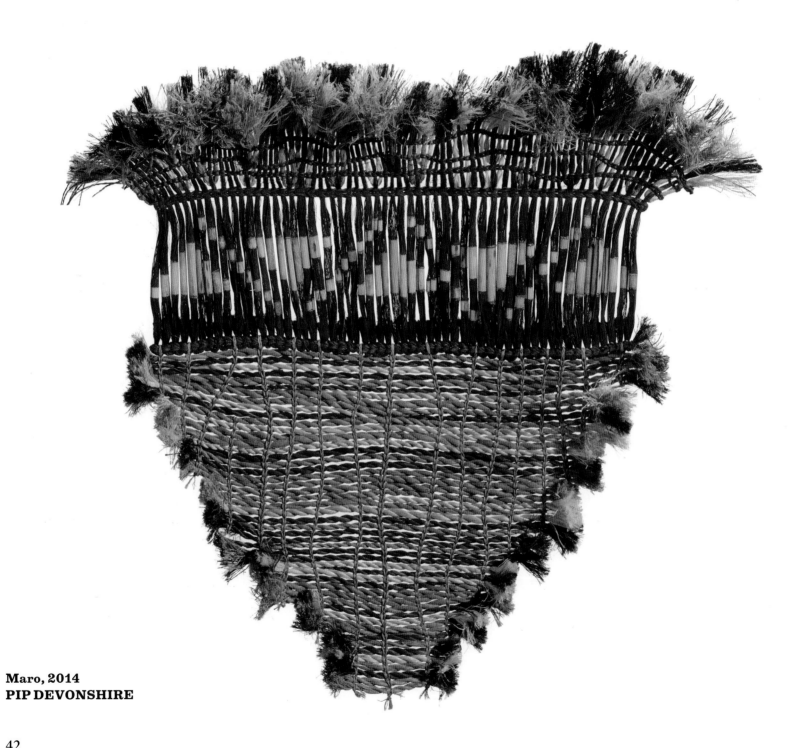

Maro, 2014
PIP DEVONSHIRE

Pip Devonshire, Weaver/Tutor

Ko Tānemahuta, nāna i tokotoko ōna Mātua kia puta tātou ki te whai ao ki te ao mārama.

This artwork is based on the story of Ranginui (sky father) and Papatūānuku (earth mother), who were entwined in an embrace so intense that their children were forced to exist in a world of darkness between them. The parents were successfully propped apart by their son Tāne.

Three divisions within the maro embody Ranginui, who stands above, Papatūanuku, who lies below, and the natural world within which we dwell. Our ancestral parents are separated by props, viewed as diagonal haehae (tears) within the triangular-shaped weaving pattern known as aronui.

Traditional style maro.

maro garment

About Maro

Traditional Māori clothing included maro, a garment worn around the waist and fastened like an apron. Traditional maro came in several different styles made from various native plant materials. One type is a maro kōpua, a thick triangular garment worn by women. The border was decorated with tāniko, a decorative geometric pattern. Long ties were wound around the waist to fasten and secure the maro in place. Another style of maro designed specifically for use by men was a maro aute made with specially prepared bark cloth from the aute tree.

Today maro are made of both traditional and contemporary materials, and still worn for important pōwhiri (welcoming ceremony) or for kapa haka (performance song and dance). Sometimes maro are made as a display piece, rather for than for use as a wearable garment.

Traditional Materials

Muka (flax fibre), native leaves, aute (bark cloth made from the paper mulberry tree).

Contemporary Materials

Recycled or found objects, plastic, cloth material, glass, metals.

43

HOW TO MAKE A ...
maro wall hanging

1

To make the triangle base, fold A4 card in half lengthways, then unfold it and rule lines from the top mid point to each corner with a pencil and ruler (see template on page 73). Cut out the triangle shape.

2

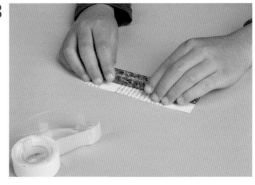

Select colourful pictures from magazines. Cut out rectangles, measuring the lengths from top to bottom of the triangle, starting from the longest point in the middle and working toward the edges.

3

To make a rolled coil, start by making a small fold in the paper and roll it over until you reach the end. Apply invisible tape to secure in place.

4

Organise the coiled rolls across the triangle base, leaving a small portion to hang over the bottom edge. Cut rolls to fit as required.

5

Once all the rolls have been placed, apply two layers of tape over the top edge.

6

Paste a length of ribbon to the top edge as a decorative addition, like the tie on a traditional maro.

The theme of this maro is garden flowers, incorporating images selected from gardening magazines.

Materials & Tools

▶ recycled magazines
▶ A4 card
▶ invisible tape
▶ pencil
▶ ruler
▶ scissors
▶ masking tape
▶ PVA glue
▶ ribbon

Alternative Materials

▶ Cut straws to length instead of rolled magazine coils.

Suggestion

▶ Choose your own theme and search out related images, for example toys, cars or colours.

Ake Ake, 2014
BRIAN FLINTOFF

Brian Flintoff, Master Carver

This porotiti was created to display the concept of the 'wind children' who take the player's thoughts and aspirations along the cords and spin them out to the world. The koru cutouts represent these ideas, and the rows of manaia (spirit faces) show them ready to leap off on their journey. I have named it *Ake Ake* because I hope that its messages go on forever.

porotiti
spinning disc

About Porotiti

Porotiti are small spinning discs that create hypnotic movements and a soothing humming sound. Porotiti are part of the taonga puoro group of Māori musical instruments. In mythology porotiti are linked with Tāwhirimātea (guardian/god of the wind). Porotiti can also be grouped in the western musical category of wind instruments.

Porotiti were often used for play by young and old alike. Although very small and quiet, porotiti can gain the attention of a group of people by focusing them intently on the object to listen for the sound. The gentle vibrations are believed to aid in soothing chest congestion.

Porotiti can be flat and circular, or in the shape of a pointed leaf. They are played by a cord looped through two holes in the centre, threaded like a button hole. The disc is centred, twirled and spun repeatedly between the hands. When not being played, they make great pendants.

Traditional Materials
Stone, bone, wood.

Contemporary Materials
Plastic, string, cardboard.

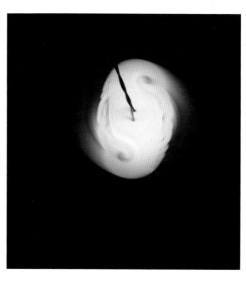

A porotiti spinning.

HOW TO MAKE A ...
porotiti spinning disc

1

Cut lengths of double-sided tape and apply to base of button.

2

Pull off the top cover to reveal the sticky surface and sprinkle with glitter, using a container to catch any excess. Apply tape one length at a time to create a criss-cross abstract pattern inspired by weaving.

3

Measure out string the length of your arms, square to the width of your shoulders, double this length again and cut the end.

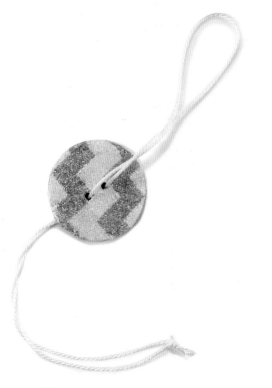

4

Thread string through the holes as pictured. Tie a firm knot to join the ends.

5

To spin, position the porotiti in the middle of the string and twirl it by winding the string in a circular motion in front of you. When it's fully wound, pull side to side continually. This continuous motion will create a humming sound.

Porotiti are fun to play with, once you get your disc spinning and humming – watch as the colours morph into each other.

Materials & Tools

▶ large button
▶ glitter
▶ double-sided tape
▶ string
▶ scissors

Alternative Materials

▶ Recycle a soft plastic jar lid instead of a button. Pierce holes 5 mm each side of the centre point, thread with string and decorate.

Suggestion

▶ Experiment with different types of string to get the best sound and spin.

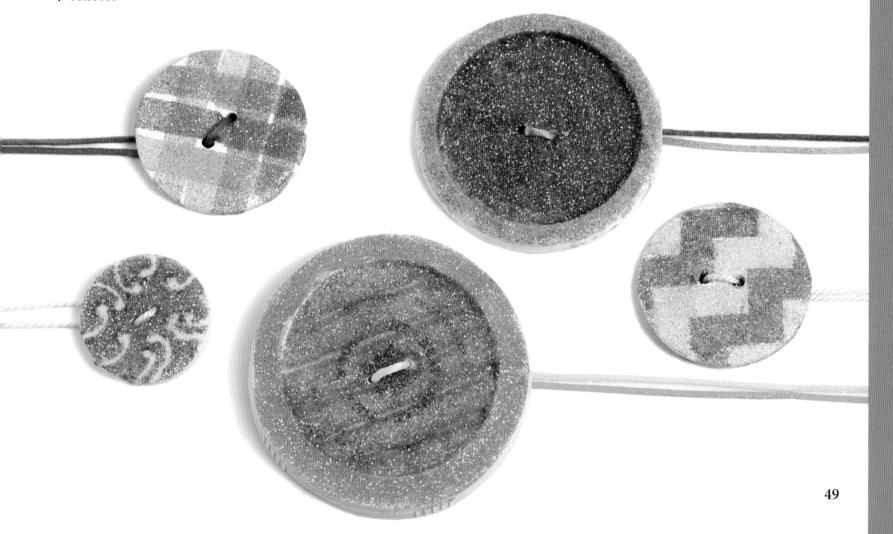

49

Wheku, 1998
ROI TOIA

Roi Toia, Sculptor/Carver

This artwork was inspired by the powerful imagery of the whale tail located in the upper centre of this carved arrangement, while an abstract face completes the mask form. It represents Kae, the infamous ancestor who killed the well-known pet whale of Tinirau. The story can be retold as an example of right and wrong.

The inspiration for this carving goes back to spending time with the celebrated carver and artist Dr Cliff Whiting. Being invited to work under Cliff on the contemporary marae project at Te Papa Tongarewa was a memorable and defining experience. The reward was experiencing how the other student artists and Cliff went about their day, producing work for the marae. Their method of constructing and adding to a carving was appealing, and led to the carving approach I have developed in recent years.

Wheku carved by
Norm Heke, 2013.

wheku mask

About Wheku

Placed at the roof gable of a meeting house is a carved face or mask that represents an important tipuna (ancestor). Traditionally the mask is carved in two different styles: the wheku style and a koruru style. The distinguishing feature that sets the two apart is that the koruru have large rounded eyes. Sometimes sitting above the wheku is the tekoteko, another type of carved figure that also represents an ancestor.

Very old carvings, including wheku, were made using stone tools such as toki (adzes) to shape and form wood and whao (chisels) to define detail. Most carvers today prefer to use electric power tools and metal chisels, although some carvers still prefer the use of traditional stone tools. It is common practice these days for student carvers to be assigned a wheku as their first project. There are symbolic meanings behind the surface patterns seen in carving, though the patterns and meanings vary from iwi to iwi.

Traditional Materials
Native timber including tōtara, rimu, pūriri and maire, with pāua for the eyes.

Contemporary Materials
Plastics, glass, stone.

51

HOW TO MAKE A ...
wheku mask

1

Flatten out the cereal box then draw a wheku design in pencil (see example template on page 75). Use an eraser to rub out any unwanted marks.

2

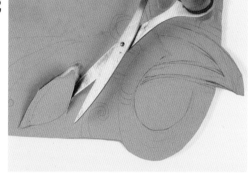

When you're satisfied with your final pencil drawing, go over the pencil lines with a marker pen.

3

Cut around the outside of the wheku, and also the inside eye areas.

4

Tape the craft stick to the back with sticky tape as a handle to hold your mask up to your face.

Make a wheku mask to wear at a fancy dress party or devise a play retelling a Māori legend.

Materials & Tools

▶ cardboard cereal box
▶ ruler
▶ pencil
▶ marker pen
▶ scissors
▶ craft stick
▶ sticky tape

Alternative Materials

▶ Use paint and apply with a fine-tipped paint brush instead of a marker pen.

Suggestion

▶ For younger children photocopy the wheku mask on page 75, scaled to the size you want. Glue to a cardboard base and decorate.

Spinning Top (Pōtaka), 2002
ROBERT JAHNKE

Robert Jahnke
Sculptor/Professor of Māori Visual Arts

Spinning Top (Pōtaka) is made out of stainless steel and was created to acknowledge the settlement of the Wellington region. It is situated in a busy lane in central Wellington, the capital city of New Zealand.

On the top face of the pōtaka are stylised designs that represent the arrival of the early Polynesian ancestors on ocean waka (canoe), the arrival of Europeans on ships and later migrants on aeroplanes.

Among the surface motifs are the Beehive building, a waka and two taniwha that legend tells formed the Wellington harbour. The artist's star sign is Aries, and zodiac signs appear on the underside of the pōtaka. One of the 12 zodiac signs is missing though, so if you have an opportunity to visit this pōtaka be a detective and try to figure out the missing sign.

Traditional style pōtaka tā and pōtaka tākiri. Digitally created replicas by Norm Heke, 2014.

pōtaka
spinning top

About Potaka

Pōtaka are spinning tops, enjoyed by children and adults in the past for fun competitive games. There are two types of Māori spinning tops in Aotearoa/New Zealand. One is a pōtaka tā (whip top) made from wood, with a separate whip (tā) that has a flax cord attached to a wooden handle. The whip was used to get the top spinning by winding the cord around the top edge of the pōtaka and skilfully launching it so that it continues to spin on the ground. Once released from the cord it could be whipped to keep spinning for as long as possible. Racing games were held over short and long distances. The prepared level surface was named the marae pōtaka (spinning top ground).

The other type is a humming top called pōtaka tākiri, which makes a humming sound when spun. Spinning games began with the word 'hei' said in unison to indicate that all competitors should start spinning. The objective was to make your top give the loudest hum and spin the longest. Traditional games like pōtaka have been reintroduced into play in more recent times.

Traditional Materials

Native timber (mataī, kahikatea, tōtara), stone, hue (gourd), shell for decoration.

Contemporary Materials

Steel, plastic, cardboard.

HOW TO MAKE A ...
pōtaka spinning top

Trace around the outside of the recycled plastic lid onto craft foam. Cut out the circle.

Decorate the circle with a marker pen.

How to spin

To spin your pōtaka hold the top of the stick between your thumb and forefinger, make a snapping motion and let it go.

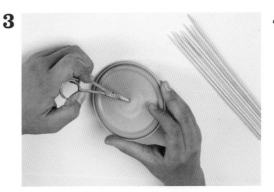

Punch a hole through the centre of the top with pointed scissors. Poke the sharp end of a bamboo skewer through the top, taking care to insert away from your hand, and trim off the excess.

Make a hole in the centre of your foam piece and thread the bamboo skewer through the foam.

These spinning tops are quick to make and easy to play with. Start up a competition with some friends to see who can make their top spin the longest.

Materials & Tools

▶ recycled plastic jar lids
▶ bamboo sticks
▶ craft foam
▶ pen
▶ felt pens
▶ nail scissors

Alternative Materials

▶ Use recycled cardboard instead of craft foam.

Suggestion

▶ Experiment with different shapes like the examples below.

Poi Girl I, 2006
ARETA WILKINSON

Areta Wilkinson, Jeweller

Artworks presented in bell jars remind us of museum exhibits, and make us think about what is important and relevant to us today. Areta Wilkinson's series of *Poi Girl* figures are silhouettes of herself, and by presenting them in this way she is questioning how Māori culture is studied and displayed in museums and art galleries. *Poi Girl* figures can also be worn as brooches as a reminder that we have a personal connection with art.

Traditional style poi.

poi
dancing ball

About Poi

Poi is the name of a performance song and dance and also the name of the object that features in the dance. There are short and long poi. Poi are swung in time to a rhythmic pattern, created through song and dance. There are examples in museums of very old ornate poi, called poi tāniko, displaying intricately woven geometric patterns. Everyday poi were made from raupō (swamp reed) for the ball and muka (flax fibre) for the plaited cord. When corn was brought to New Zealand, poi balls were made from corn husks connected to a muka cord.

Anyone of any age can play with poi for fun and entertainment, and they are useful for developing good coordination skills, flexibility and strength. Long poi are most suitable for making long swinging movements, while short poi can be used to pat back and forth in time to music or to make up your own rhythm. These days coordinated poi dances are performed by groups of women and girls, with either single or double poi. Performers practise for many hours to perfect their skill for important occasions or competitions.

Traditional Materials

Raupō, raupō flower down (for the poi filling), muka, corn husk.

Contemporary Materials

Synthetic fabrics, plastic, wool, polyester fibre pillow filling.

HOW TO MAKE A ...
poi dancing ball

1

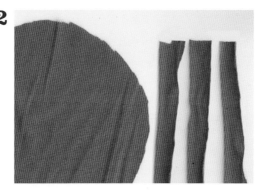

Flatten out the T-shirt. Following measurements from the poi template on page 73, use a marker pen and ruler to draw out patterns, tracing around the circular plate to make a circle. Cut out the shapes.

2

To make the poi cord, knot the three longest strips together at one end and tape the knotted end to a flat surface. Start plaiting by laying outer strands into the middle, alternating from side to side.

3

Stop plaiting the poi cord approximately 10 cm from the end, and tie it off with a knot.

4

To make the inside of the ball, tie the loose ends of the plaited cord around the pillow filling, securing them with a firm knot.

5

Lay out the material circle and place pillow filling in the middle. Pull up the fabric around the filling to make a ball, while tightly winding the small material strip around the top of the ball several times. Secure it with a double knot.

6

Draw patterns on your poi with a fabric marker pen to individualise your poi with a symbol you like.

These poi are quite durable and lovely and soft to play with.

Materials & Tools

▶ recycled cotton T-shirt
▶ pillow filling
▶ circular plate
▶ ruler, marker pen
▶ scissors, tape
▶ fabric pen (optional)

Alternative Materials

▶ Cover the outside with plastic to make a loud sound when patting poi against your hands.

Suggestion

▶ Swing your poi in time to music or while singing a song.

Manu Tangata, 2010
JAMES WEBSTER

James Webster
Carver/Ta Moko Artist/Performer

This type of kite is called a manu tangata. The main components that make up this kite are wooden dowelling for the frame and raupō leaf overlaid on the surface area and bound to the dowelling base. The mask has a papier mâché base, painted over with acrylic paint. The bird feathers on the outer edges of the kite are karoro (seagull), and the feathers surrounding the mask are albatross, bound with reed wax cord.

This kite was one of a series that I constructed for the simple reason that I became interested in them. That interest led to further research into Māori kite making, and part of my investigation was to actually construct and fly a variety of kites to learn more about them. This particular kite flies really well!

manu tukutuku kite

Traditional style manu taratahi. Digitally created replica by Norm Heke, 2014.

About Manu Tukutuku

Kites have been around for thousands of years, appearing in most ancient cultures, and kite flying has always been a popular pastime for Māori, young and old. The general name given to Māori kites is manu tukutuku. Manu taratahi are a variety of kite mostly used for play, as the lightweight plant materials and the simple triangular design meant they were easy to construct and fly. Different types of kites were flown for ceremonial purposes, or to celebrate special occasions, including Matariki, the Māori New Year occurring around May or June each year at the appearance of the Matariki star cluster.

Existing examples of large kites stored in museums are manu aute and manu tukutuku, which show a high level of craftsmanship and are of such a large scale that they would require a group of people to fly them. Some take the form of a stylised bird or human, which sometimes had the face painted with natural paint pigments.

Traditional Materials

Raupō (swamp reeds), toetoe (grass), harakeke (flax), kareao (supplejack), mānuka, kānuka, native bird feathers, black pigment, red pigment, aute (bark cloth).

Contemporary Materials

Plastic, nylon material, tape, string.

HOW TO MAKE A ...
manu tukutuku kite

1

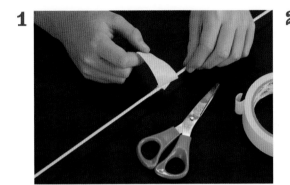

Tape two bamboo sticks together to make one long one. Make three of these.

2

Lay out the sticks in a triangle, and bind each of the three corners with tape.

3

Flatten the plastic bag, place your triangle over the top and mark with a pen around the edges, leaving a margin of 5 cm or more, then cut out the shape.

4

Choose a design to decorate the plastic using colourful marker pens. This pattern, shown on page 37, is called Poutama.

5

Attach string to the kite as shown in the image above. To make the tail, attach a piece of string (approximately 60 cm) halfway across the bottom of the kite, and add feathers to the string. Tape a small bunch of feathers to the corners of the kite as well.

6

Fold the edges of the plastic triangle over the sides of the kite and join with clear tape.

This type of kite is a similar shape to a manu taratahi. Find a large, open outside space to fly your kite on a windy day.

Materials & Tools

- recycled plastic bag
- bamboo sticks
- marker pens
- scissors
- tape
- invisible tape
- string
- feathers

Alternative Materials

- Upcycle lightweight vinyl material instead of plastic. Use heavy-duty tape to secure it to the frame or sew it on.

Suggestion

- Kites can be tricky to get flying, you may need to adjust the placement of the string or the tail to get it flying well.

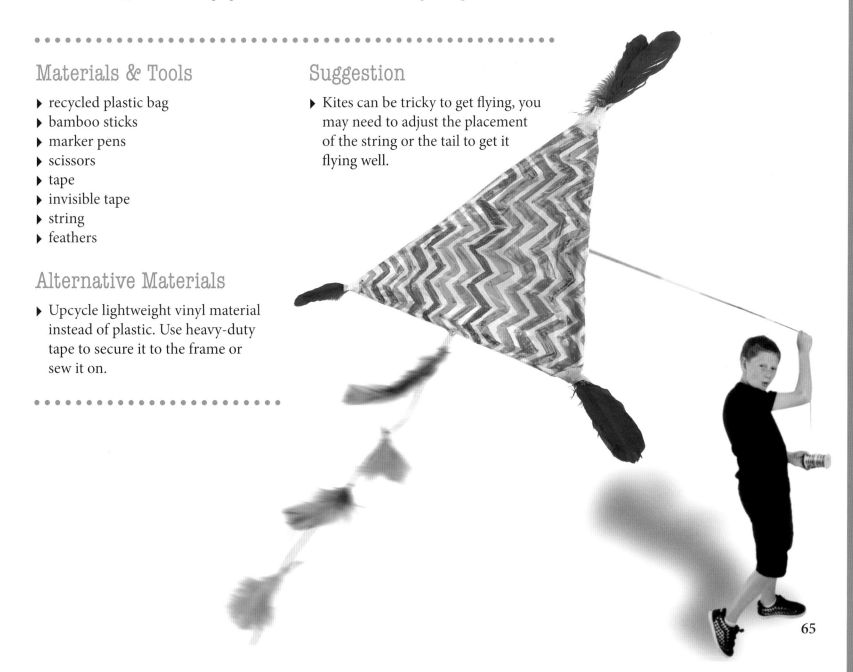

kaimahi toi kōrero artist biographies

TODD COUPER
Rongomaiwahine, Ngāti Kahungunu

I was born in 1974 in the small East Coast town of Wairoa and I am of Rongomaiwahine, Ngāti Kahungunu descent. Growing up as a youngster I was always interested in art and was fascinated with the carvings and kōwhaiwhai patterns in the wharenui. I would spend hours doing pencil sketches and drawings and found that my passion for art grew as I got older. At Te Aute College my art teacher Mark Dashper gave me great encouragement to further my art studies and so I went on to do the Diploma of Art, Craft and Design Māori at Waiariki Polytechnic in Rotorua. This is where I was exposed to all kinds of art and learnt many new skills including whakairo (wood carving). Once I was introduced to whakairo I knew quickly that this was something I wanted to pursue.

In my final year of study I met Roi Toia, who was then my carving tutor. After graduating in 1995 Roi invited me to work alongside him in his workshop and this formed a partnership that would see us working together for the next 17 years. Initially under Roi's guidance I would later develop my own style of carving. I now continue to create artworks that echo my inner thoughts and ideas. These concepts are then given an added substance being interwoven with different aspects of the deep, diverse and rich culture of Maori.

PIP DEVONSHIRE

Weaving is a continuous activity, as often as possible designing, preparing and meticulously creating. Our tūpuna have gifted to us an incredible wealth of weaving intricacies and processes, styles, forms, techniques and tikanga. From within this mātauranga Pip has defined her own unique style by considering alternative ways of presenting woven form and technique. She descends from a long line of weavers whose innovativeness inherently informs her weaving exploration.

BRIAN FLINTOFF

Brian Flintoff's work is exhibited and held in private and public collections worldwide. He became known for his bone carvings, and later for his creation of taonga puoro as he worked with Dr Hirini Melbourne, who led Te Haumanu, a group dedicated to the revival of Māori flute and instrument making and playing.

Support and guidance from the Māori community has been the greatest influence and inspiration for his carving. Therefore he considers the most satisfying acknowledgement possible is that he is proud to have many pieces 'at home' on marae throughout Aotearoa/ New Zealand.

LEWIS TAMIHANA GARDINER
Te Arawa, Ngāti Awa, Te Whanau a Apanui, Ngāi Tahu

Lewis Gardiner is regarded as one of the most innovative and respected Māori jade artists of his generation. His work is highly sought after by art collectors in New Zealand, Europe, Asia, Australia and the United States. He studied Māori Craft and Design at Waiariki Institute of Technology in Rotorua, graduating in 1994. In 1995 he became a full-time jade and bone carver, specialising in traditional Māori imagery. Knowledge gained from visiting a master jade carver in China in 2003 further enhanced his skill and ability working in large-scale sculpture and fine detail. He participated in Kiwa–Pacific Connections in Vancouver, Canada in 2003.

Recognised for his innovative approach to design style and composition, he received the Mana Pounamu Award for contemporary Māori jade design in 1999, 2001 and 2003. He was appointed as the inaugural Head of Department of Te Takapū O Rotowhio (the National Stone and Bone Carving School) at the New Zealand Māori Arts and Crafts Institute in Rotorua in 2003, where he worked for several years. Lewis is now a dedicated full-time artist.

KOHAI GRACE
Ngāti Toa Rangatira, Ngāti Porou

Kohai believes her interest in Māori art stemmed from childhood, having been taken along by her parents to the Māori Artist and Writers conferences that were held annually on marae around the country during the 1970s. In 1986 Kohai studied on a weaving course held at the Wellington Art Centre, and has been weaving ever since. Over the years she has produced work for various commissions, hapū and iwi projects, fashion shows, exhibitions and collections held nationally and internationally, and has also completed tukutuku (lattice panel work) for her own wharenui (meeting house) at Hongoeka Marae.

Further study of weaving and art continued at Te Wananga-o-Raukawa, and she gained a degree in Māori Design and Art under master weaver and carver Erenora and Rangi Puketapu-Hetet, before completing the Master of Māori Visual Arts at Massey University under Robert Jahnke. Kohai has taught weaving and tukutuku at a number of educational institutions around New Zealand, including a long-term director's and teaching position for the degree programme at Te Wānanga-o-Raukawa.

NORM HEKE
Ngā Puhi, Ngāti Kahu, Te Arawa

Norm was born in Taranaki. His formative years were spent growing up on farms in the North Island, but at the age of 12 he moved with his family to Wellington, where he has lived ever since. His early experiences of farming life taught him resourcefulness, resilience and the Kiwi 'can do' attitude, an approach he applies to all his projects. Influential people in his early career included Alwyn (Hop) Owen, who encouraged Norm to study photography as a professional. Later, as a graduate photographer working with Terry Crowe in his Wellington studio, he learned the value of thinking outside of the square.

Norm is a photographer and digital artist who works as an imaging specialist at Te Papa, where his photography and short documentary films have featured in numerous museum exhibitions. He has worked with many of New Zealand's leading contemporary artists and his imagery has appeared in a number of award-winning art publications. Norm's first solo exhibition was *OMGs: Maori Gods in the 21st Century* (2011), encompassing his passion for Māori history and traditions, the natural environment and photorealism.

AMORANGI HIKUROA
Ngā Puhi, Ngāti Maniapoto

Amorangi Hikuroa lives in Whangārei and is a member of Ngā Kaihanga Uku (Māori Clay Workers Collective). For Amorangi the medium of clay is a very powerful alchemy, in which the sculptor inherently wields all the elements required to create. Influential to his work is Te Ao Māori (the Māori world), and the ceramic histories of the ancient peoples for whom uku (clay) has had a part to play for thousands of years. This includes the tangata whenua (indigenous people) of America, Africa, Europe, Asia and all the way back to the Jomon people of ancient Japan who lived around 6000 BC.

ROBERT JAHNKE
Ngāi Taharora, Te Whanau a Iritekura, Te Whanau a Rakairoa o Ngāti Porou

Robert Jahnke is a teacher and an artist. He has illustrated children's books, including *The House of the People* about building a carved Māori house, and *The Fish of our Fathers*, written by Ron Bacon, about building a Māori war canoe. He has also created animated films such as *Te Utu: The Battle of the Gods* in the National Film Archives Collection about the battle of the children of Ranginui, the sky father and Papatūānuku, the earth mother. He has taught at intermediate and secondary schools, and now teaches art at Massey University in Palmerston North, where he is Professor of Māori Visual Arts.

SONIA SNOWDEN
Ngāti Hine, Ngāti Wai, Ngāti Whātua, Ngā Puhi

'Sonia is a highly respected weaver from Ōtaki. "A Sonia Snowden Kete" is now uttered like a revered brand name. Over the years, Sonia Snowden has created a severely poetic repertoire of finely woven kete whakairo, of beautifully executed tukutuku panels and kākahu. But it's the resonance of her extraordinarily fine kete whakairo which invites you, the viewer to experience the beauty and soul of her work which transports you into an unexpected spiralling, spiritual journey … for each kete whakairo resonates with the nearly forgotten beauty of our past, of humble stories of loss, of gain, of feelings and above all, of love and compassion for the humble kete of our whaea tupuna.'

Diane Prince 2011

NGĀTAI TAEPA
Te Arawa and Te Āti Awa

I whanau mai a Ngātai ki Whakatiki ki Te Whanganui-a-Tara i te tau 1976. Kei te noho ia ki Te Papaioea, ā, he mahi anō tāna hoki ki te Pūtahi-ā-Toi hei kaiako. Ko tōna kuia me tōna pāpā he mātanga toi. Nā rāua ia i whakatupu ki ngā ahuatanga o te ao toi. I ngākaunui a Ngātai ki ngā mahi toi i a ia e kura ana ki Te Aute Kāreti. I a ia te honore nui kia mātakitaki, kia hāpai hoki i te waihanga o ngā kōwhaiwhai mō Te Whare o Rangi i raro i ngā whakaakoranga o tētahi kaiako toi rongonui a Mark Dashper.

Ka whāia tonutia a Ngātai te mahi toi ki Te Kūnenga ki Pūrehuroa ki Te Papaioea i te taha o ngā mātanga toi a Robert Jahnke, Kura Te Waru-Rewiri rātou ko Shane Cotton. I mutu a Ngātai i tōna tohu Paetahi mō ngā mahi toi i te tau 2000, katahi ko tōna tohu Paerua mō nga mahi toi i te tau 2003, ā, kua riro i a ia he tūranga kaiako ki te taha tohu Paetahi mahi toi.

Ngātai Taepa was born in Upper Hutt, in 1976. He lives in Palmerston North and works at Te Pūtahi-ā-Toi (School of Māori Art, Knowledge and Education) Massey University. Both his grandmother and father are artists so he was brought up with the arts as a part of his everyday life. Ngātai was passionate about art during his time at Te Aute College. He was fortunate in that during his time at Te Aute he witnessed the building of the college meeting house, Te Whare o Rangi, and he helped paint the kōwhaiwhai panels under the tutelage of renowned art teacher, Mark Dashper.

Ngātai carried on his pursuit of art at Massey University, Palmerston North, under the guidance of artists such as Robert Jahnke, Kura Te Waru-Rewiri and Shane Cotton. He completed his Bachelor of Māori Visual Arts in 2000 and his Masters in Māori Visual Arts in 2003, and is now a lecturer in the Bachelor of Māori Visual Arts programme at Massey University.

ROI TOIA
Ngā Puhi

Working for more than 30 years in the art of whakairo, Roi has forged a carving style and reputation that finds his work profiled in many forums. His inspiration has always been sourced from a traditional, natural viewpoint. However having a 'visual voice' that reflects today is equally important to him. With the wisdom and lessons of the past, he finds material to set a platform in order to say something about today.

JAMES WEBSTER
Tainui, Te Arawa, Pākehā

James Webster is based in the town of Coromandel. He has worked in the arts industry for over 20 years as a freelance multidisciplinary artist, specialising in sculpture and working in the fields of carving (bone, stone and wood), painting and other mixed-media creations.

As owner/operator of the Tahaa, Tāmoko and Māori Arts studio, James works as a tāmoko (Māori tattoo) artist. He is also a maker, player and performer of taonga puoro (Māori musical instruments). He acquired a Studio Certificate from Toihoukura, Te Tairawhiti Polytechnic, Gisborne in 1998. He has a Bachelor of Arts Te Maunga Kura Toi (with excellence) in whakairo rākau (Māori wood carving) from Te Wananga o Aotearoa, gained in 2005 under the tutelage of Dr Paakaariki Harrison and Professor Kereti Rautangata.

WENDY WHITEHEAD
Ngāti Porou

I love working on a small scale, mainly with metal, stone and fibre. I like working with new materials and pushing their qualities, and enjoy the challenge of the creative process. My work is inspired by life in general and is often based within my Māori culture. From a young age I enjoyed making things, so my parents supported this and encouraged me to experiment. I have worked in the public sector, tutored in art media at a number of educational institutions, and now run my own art education business. My business enables me to make a living out of my passion for art, while sharing the knowledge and expertise I have gained with my students.

As an artist I have participated in exhibitions, symposia, collaborations and hui (gatherings), both nationally and internationally. I feel greatly honoured to have received recognition for my work, and this has encouraged me to strive higher to acknowledge those that tautoko (support) me along my path. I am part of a network of artists walking a similar journey, and I feel humbled to call them my peers.

DR CLIFF WHITING
Te Whānau-ā-Apanui

Originally from Te Kaha on New Zealand's East Coast, Cliff's artistic talent was evident from an early age. In his formative years as an artist he was greatly influenced by Pine Taiapa of Ngāti Porou, and E. Mervyn Taylor, a print-maker, painter and sculptor who invited him to live at his family home in Wellington while attending teachers' college, from whom he learnt a great deal. Gordon Tovey was a significant influence in the area of art education. Elements of Te Ao Māori and Te Whānau-ā-Apanui traditions permeate the work he has produced from a range of disciplines including carving, sculpture, drawing, print-making, painting, weaving and photography. His innovative techniques and approach to materials have inspired many New Zealand artists.

As the first Kaihautū (leader) of the Museum of New Zealand Te Papa Tongarewa, he set the foundation for biculturalism, a vision he embodied in the iconic Marae Rongomaraeroa. His significant contribution to marae building and renovation, services in art education and administration have earned prestigious honours including The Order of New Zealand for services to the arts in 1998 and the Arts Foundation of New Zealand Icon Award in 2013.

ARETA WILKINSON
Ngāi Tahu

Exploring Areta Wilkinson's work, whether it is a survey, a series or a single object, is always a journey through her life history and Ngāi Tahu cultural landscapes. Jewellery is the embodiment of personal and collective stories. Wearable Māori taonga are more than just ornaments to adorn the body, they are connections to the land, the gods, history and legend. They facilitate relationships, identities, politics and ethics.

Areta's practice extends over 20 years, and her work is seen in national public galleries and collections such as the 3rd Auckland Triennial, City Gallery Wellington, Auckland Museum, Dowse Art Museum and the Museum of New Zealand Te Papa Tongarewa. She has been a design lecturer in jewellery from 1995 to 2008, and currently lives in North Canterbury at Oxford, near the foothills of the Southern Alps.

ngā tātauira templates

Hei Tiki Neck Pendant

Karu Eyes
Ihu Nose
Waha Mouth

Ringaringa
Arms & hands

Waewae
Legs & feet

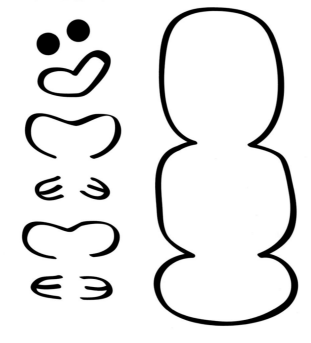

Tinana Body

Koru Spiral Form

Koru can be developed in different ways; here are a few ideas.

Poupou Figures

These examples give an indication of regional differences in carving styles, each iwi has their own distinctive style.

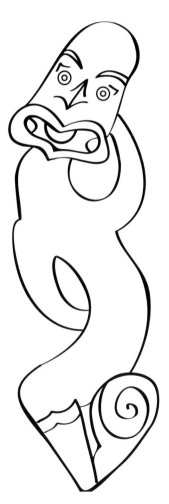

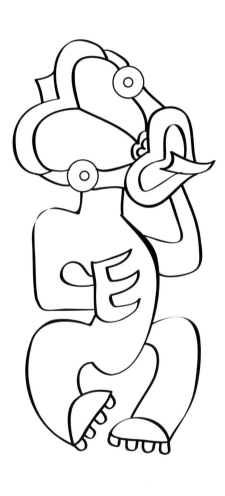

Gisborne

Hokianga/Kaipara

Bay of Plenty

Kōwhaiwhai Scroll Patterns

Patterns from left to right:

Pātikitiki (diamond-shaped design)
Kaperua (symbolic of things doubled)
Kōwhai ngutukākā (rare endemic plant)

Maro Wall Hanging

Length = 297 mm

Length = 255 mm

Length = 255 mm

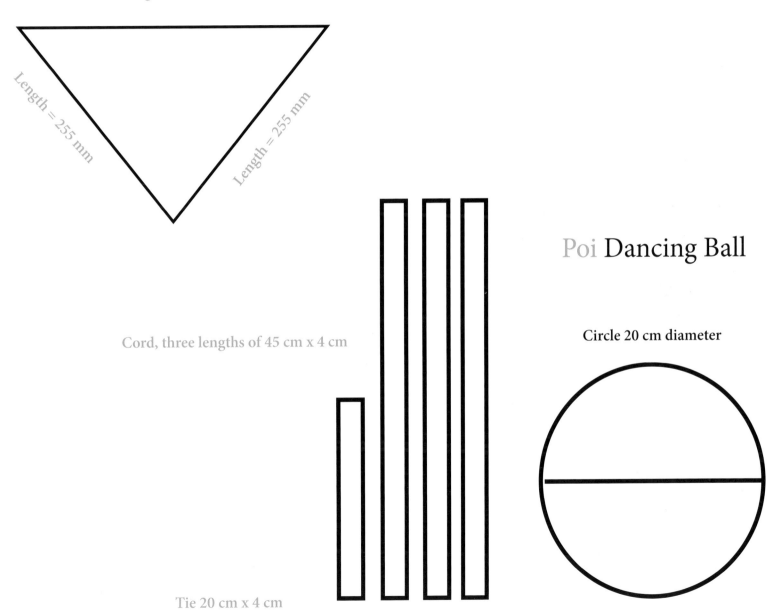

Cord, three lengths of 45 cm x 4 cm

Tie 20 cm x 4 cm

Poi Dancing Ball

Circle 20 cm diameter

Waka Huia Treasure Box

Selection of abstracted whakairo (carving) pattern motifs, for stamp designs.

Koru spiral form

Pākati dog's tooth

Unaunahi fish scales

Wheku Mask

Papakupu Māori Glossary

Aotearoa New Zealand
Atua god, supernatural being, deity
Aute mulberry tree bark cloth

Haehae cut up, lacerate, tear
Hapū sub-tribe
Harakeke New Zealand flax, *Phormium tenax*
Hei tiki neck pendant
Heke rafters
Heru comb
Hine-te-iwa-iwa goddess
Houhere lacebark, *Hoheria populnea*
Hue bottle gourd, *Lagenaria siceraria*
Huia extinct bird species, *Heteralocha acutirostris*

Ipu container
Iwi tribe

Kahikatea tall swamp tree, *Dacrycarpus dacrydioides*
Kākaho flower stalk of toetoe
Kānuka white tea tree, *Kunzea ericoides*
Kapa haka performance song and dance
Kape crescent moon shape with regularly spaced circles
Kareao supplejack, *Ripogonum scandens*
Kauri New Zealand's largest native tree, *Agathis australis*
Kete basket or handbag
Kete tāniko geometric patterning
Kete whakairo ornate finely woven basket
Kiekie vine species, *Freycinetia baueriana* subsp. *banksi*
Koru spiral form

Koruru carved representation of a human face with large rounded eyes
Kōwhaiwahai painted scroll pattern
Kumete wooden serving bowl
Kuta sedge species, *Eleocharis sphacelata*

Maire broadleaf tree, *Nestegis cunninghamii*
Manu taratahi triangular kite
Mānuka tea tree, *Leptospermum scoparium*
Māori indigenous person of Aotearoa/New Zealand
Maro waist garment
Maro aute bark cloth garment for men
Maro kōpua women's triangular waist garment
Matāi podocarp tree, *Prumnopitys taxifolia*
Matariki Māori New Year
Muka processed flax fibre

Ngāti Porou East Coast tribal group

Paru natural black mud used to dye flax
Pātaka storehouse
Pātiki flounder, diamond shape pattern
Pātua food dish made from bark
Pāua abalone, *Haliotis* spp.
Pīngao golden sand sedge, *Desmoschoenus spiralis*
Pītau spiral
Poi dancing ball
Poi tāniko ornate poi
Porotiti spinning disc
Pōtaka spinning top
Pōtaka tā whip top
Pōtaka tākiri a top that makes a humming sound
Pounamu greenstone or nephrite

Poupou carved wall panel

Poutama stairway step pattern

Pōwhiri welcoming ceremony

Pūriri tree species, *Vitex lucens*

Raranga weave or plait

Raupō bulrush, *Typha orientalis*

Rimu podocarp tree, *Dacrydium cupressinum*

Ruarua whetū double star

Tā flax whip

Tahā gourd

Tāhuhu ridgepole

Taioma white clay

Tāne Mahuta guardian/god of the forest and birds

Tangaroa guardian/god of the ocean

Tangata whenua indigenous people of the land

Tāniko decorative geometric border pattern

Taonga treasured possessions

Taonga puoro Māori musical instruments

Tapu sacred

Tāwhirimātea guardian/god of the wind

Tekoteko carved ancestral figure above the apex of a meeting house

Tī kōuka cabbage tree, *Cordyline australis*

Tiki the original ancestor

Tīpuna ancestors (eastern dialect)

Toetoe grass species, *Cortaderia* spp.

Toki adze

Tōtara podocarp tree, *Podocarpus cunninghamii*

Tukutuku lattice wall panel

Tūpuna ancestors (western dialect)

Uku clay

Waka canoe

Waka huia feather box

Whakairo carving

Whakapapa genealogy

Whao chisel

Whare tīpuna ancestral meeting house

Wharenui meeting house

Wheku carved representation of a human face

Craft Glossary

Bling shiny decorative craft pieces

Clay fine-grained earth that can be moulded into pottery and ceramics

Diamantés imitation diamonds made of plastic

Embroider decorate cloth by sewing on a pattern

Graphic relating to visual art, especially drawing, engraving and lettering

Image representing the external form of a person or object

Lattice a structure composed of wood or metal strips crossed and fastened together

Masking tape adhesive tape used when painting to cover areas on which paint is not required

Oil paint paint with the pigment suspended in oil

PVA polyvinyl acetate, also known as white craft glue and school glue

Quill the hollow centre shaft of a feather

Recycle conversion of waste products into reusable material

Sculpture the art of making a three-dimensional representation or abstract form

Stitch a loop created from a threaded needle

Text written or printed words

Image Credits

page 6

Wendy Whitehead
Te Heru o Te Kooti 2012
Wood, sterling silver, pure silver,
copper, glass, rubber
210 x 70 x 10 mm

page 10

Todd Couper
Waka Maumahara 2014
Wood
270 x 160 mm

page 11

Waka huia, 1800–1900
Photographed by Norm Heke
Courtesy of the Museum of New Zealand
Te Papa Tongarewa
ME002370

page 14

Dr Cliff Whiting
Te Wehenga o Rangi rāua ko Papa 1975
Mixed media mural
7075 x 2590 mm
Collection of the National Library of
New Zealand
Image supplied by the National Library of
New Zealand

page 15

Hone Ngatoto
Te Aitanga-a-Hauiti, Tolaga Bay
Poupou, 1881
Photographed by Michael Hall
Courtesy of the Museum of New Zealand
Te Papa Tongarewa
ME000954

page 18

Sonia Snowden
Kete Whakairo 2003
Harakeke (flax), muka (processed flax fibre)
350 x 300 mm

page 22

Ngātai Taepa
Tinakori 2006
Solvent paint, wood, PVC pipe
1465 x 335 x 210 mm

page 23

Kōwhaiwhai pattern, 1800–1900
Photographed by Norm Heke
Courtesy of the Museum of New Zealand
Te Papa Tongarewa

page 26

Amorangi Hikuroa
Ipu Kākano (seed vessel) 2014
Clay
110 x 140 mm

page 30

Norm Heke
Hinetītama 2011
Digital photograph
1800 x 1400 mm

page 34

Kohai Grace
Pātikitiki 2013
Kiekie, pink chemical dye, rimu, pine
725 x 325 x 45 mm

page 35

Ngāti Whātua rākei
Tukutuku panel
Photographed by Michael Hall
Courtesy of the Museum of New Zealand
Te Papa Tongarewa and the
Ngāti Whātua o Ōrākei Trust
ME014017

pages 38–39

Lewis Gardiner
Hei Tiki I 2013
Pounamu
90 x 50 mm

Hei Tiki II 2013
Pounamu
100 x 60 mm

page 42

Pip Devonshire
Maro 2014
Muka (processed flax fibre)
290 x 300 mm

page 43

Tūhoe
Maro
Photographed by Norm Heke
Courtesy of the Museum of New Zealand
Te Papa Tongarewa
ME000773

page 46

Brian Flintoff
Ake Ake 2014
Beef bone
85 x 50 x 10 mm

Acknowledgements

We are extremely grateful to the artists, for joining us on the journey to create this resource to open up the world of Maori art for children. Your works of art form the heart of this book: Todd Couper, Pip Devonshire, Brian Flintoff, Lewis Gardiner, Kohai Grace, Norm Heke, Amorangi Hikuroa, Robert Jahnke, Sonia Snowden, Ngātai Taepa, Roi Toia, James Webster, Wendy Whitehead, Dr Cliff Whiting, Areta Wilkinson

To the wonderful children and parents, it was great fun working with you all modelling for other kids how to make the activities: Aasia Noanoa, Selina Burt, Jamie Locke-Weir, Shaolin Paul, Alma Paul, Kaia Kemp, Edison Raki-Noanoa, Tiana Weepu, Randall whānau (Hanna, Renee, Awa, Evie, Jack), Andre Rasmussen, Bella Carlyle, Hanah Fluery, Tahu Ross, Hinetītama image, left to right: Hinewaipounamu Rangihuna, Mere Boynton, Te Koha Noanoa

The time, expertise and feedback of the following people has been invaluable: Dougal Austin, Curator Māori – Museum of New Zealand Te Papa Tongarewa; Dylan Owen, National Adviser – National Library of New Zealand; Paora Tibble, Kaituhi reo Māori – Museum of New Zealand Te Papa Tongarewa; Peter Ireland, Exhibitions Manager – National Library of New Zealand; Mark Adams, Photographer; Linda Fordyce and Margaret Tolland – Pātaka Art + Museum Education; Kura Gallery, Auckland

To Robbie Burton and the team at Craig Potton Publishing, thank you for believing in us and the value of this resource to Aotearoa/New Zealand.

page 50
Roi Toia
Wheku 1998
Mataī, jarrah burl, pounamu, stain
660 x 445 x 90 mm

page 51
Norm Heke
Wheku, 2013
Tōtara, pāua
350 x 200 mm

page 54
Robert Jahnke
Spinning Top (Pōtaka) 2002
Stainless steel
3500 x 2900 mm

page 58
Areta Wilkinson
Poi Girl I 2006
Monel 400, 9 carat gold pin, brass, paint, wood, glass, felt brooch
200 x 270 x 200 mm
Image by Mark Adams

page 59
Poi
Photographed by Mike O'Neill
Courtesy of the Museum of New Zealand
Te Papa Tongarewa
ME011443

page 63
James Webster
Manu Tangata 2010
Wooden dowelling, raupō leaf, papier mâché, feathers
Approx. 1500 x 1700 mm

About the authors

Julie Noanoa (Te Aitanga a Hauiti Iwi) has a background teaching in primary schools, and has years of experience working as an education specialist at City Gallery Wellington, Pataka Art + Museum and Te Papa, teaching and developing online learning resources. She has a diploma in graphic design and recently started postgraduate study in education at Victoria University.

Norm Heke (Ngāpuki, Ngati Kahu, Te Arawa Iwi) is a photographer and digital artist who works as an imaging specialist at Te Papa, where his photography and short documentary films have featured in numerous museum exhibitions. He has worked with many of New Zealand's leading contemporary artists on several art publications, and his imagery has appeared in a number of award-winning publications. Norm's first solo exhibition was *OMGs: Māori Gods in the 21st Century* (2011), encompassing his passion for Māori history and traditions, the natural environment and photorealism.

First published in 2014 by Craig Potton Publishing

Craig Potton Publishing
98 Vickerman Street, PO Box 555, Nelson, New Zealand
www.craigpotton.co.nz

© Julie Noanoa and Norm Heke

Paperback ISBN: 978-1-927213-13-1
Hardback ISBN: 978-1-927213-14-8

Printed in China by Midas Printing International Ltd